AF228620

WISCONSIN

BY RYAN GALE

CONTENT CONSULTANT
Patricia Stovey, PhD
Assistant Professor of History
University of Wisconsin-La Crosse

An Imprint of Abdo Publishing
abdobooks.com

abdobooks.com

Published by Abdo Publishing, a division of ABDO, PO Box 398166, Minneapolis, Minnesota 55439. Copyright © 2023 by Abdo Consulting Group, Inc. International copyrights reserved in all countries. No part of this book may be reproduced in any form without written permission from the publisher. Core Library™ is a trademark and logo of Abdo Publishing.

Printed in the United States of America, North Mankato, Minnesota
052022
092022

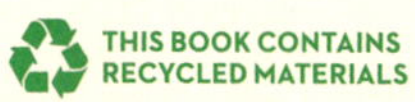

Cover Photo: Shutterstock Images, map and icons; Shane Sabin/Shutterstock Images, deer
Interior Photos: Lorraine Swanson/Shutterstock Images, 4–5; Red Line Editorial, 8 (Wisconsin), 8 (USA); Ken Duffney/Shutterstock Images, 10–11; Sean Pavone/Shutterstock Images, 13, 45; Lukasz Stefanski/Shutterstock Images, 16 (flag); Tom Reichner/Shutterstock Images, 16 (badger); Jayne Gulbrand/Shutterstock Images, 16 (bird); Radomir Rezny/Alamy, 16 (dog); Paul Reeves Photography/Shutterstock Images, 16 (flower); Shutterstock Images, 20–21, 24, 43; David R. Frazier/Science Source, 26; Michael Tatman/Shutterstock Images, 28–29; iStockphoto, 31; Jayne Lipkovich/Shutterstock Images, 34–35; Roberto Galan/Shutterstock Images, 36; David Stluka/AP Images, 38; Eric Miller/Reuters/Newscom, 41

Editor: Marie Pearson
Series Designer: Joshua Olson

Library of Congress Control Number: 2021951570

Publisher's Cataloging-in-Publication Data

Names: Gale, Ryan, author.
Title: Wisconsin / by Ryan Gale
Description: Minneapolis, Minnesota : Abdo Publishing, 2023 | Series: Core library of US states | Includes online resources and index.
Identifiers: ISBN 9781532197925 (lib. bdg.) | ISBN 9781098270681 (ebook)
Subjects: LCSH: U.S. states--Juvenile literature. | Midwest States--Juvenile literature. | Wisconsin--History--Juvenile literature. | Physical geography--United States--Juvenile literature.
Classification: DDC 977.5--dc23

Population demographics broken down by race and ethnicity come from the 2019 census estimate. Population totals come from the 2020 census.

CONTENTS

THE BADGER STATE

Clear water ripples as a boat slowly navigates a narrow, winding river. The passengers gaze at amazing sandstone cliffs formed by rushing water and wind over thousands of years. The moss-covered formations are almost close enough to touch. Wisconsin Dells is a town located along the Wisconsin River in the central part of the state. A dell is a small, forested passage of land cut by water. Wisconsin Dells is one of Wisconsin's most famous places.

People enjoy seeing the sandstone cliffs of the dells in Wisconsin.

People have visited its unique land formations since the 1800s. They enjoyed the shapes of the sandstone cliffs rising from the river. Today the town is also home to the nation's largest water park. The Noah's Ark water park includes 70 acres (28 ha) of swimming pools, artificial streams, and waterslides. Wisconsin Dells is known as the water park capital of the world.

ABOUT WISCONSIN

Wisconsin is part of the Midwest region of the United States. The state is bordered by Minnesota and Iowa to the west, Illinois to the south, and Michigan to the north.

Lake Michigan makes up the state's eastern border. Lake Superior borders the state in the northwest.

Wisconsin is known as the Badger State. A badger is a member of the skunk and weasel family. It uses its claws to dig burrows in the ground. Early miners in Wisconsin used to dig caves to live in during the winter. This reminded people of badgers. They began calling the miners badgers, and the name stuck. Wisconsin is also known as America's Dairyland for its many dairy farms.

MAP OF
WISCONSIN

This map shows several locations in Wisconsin. How does it help you better understand Chapter One?

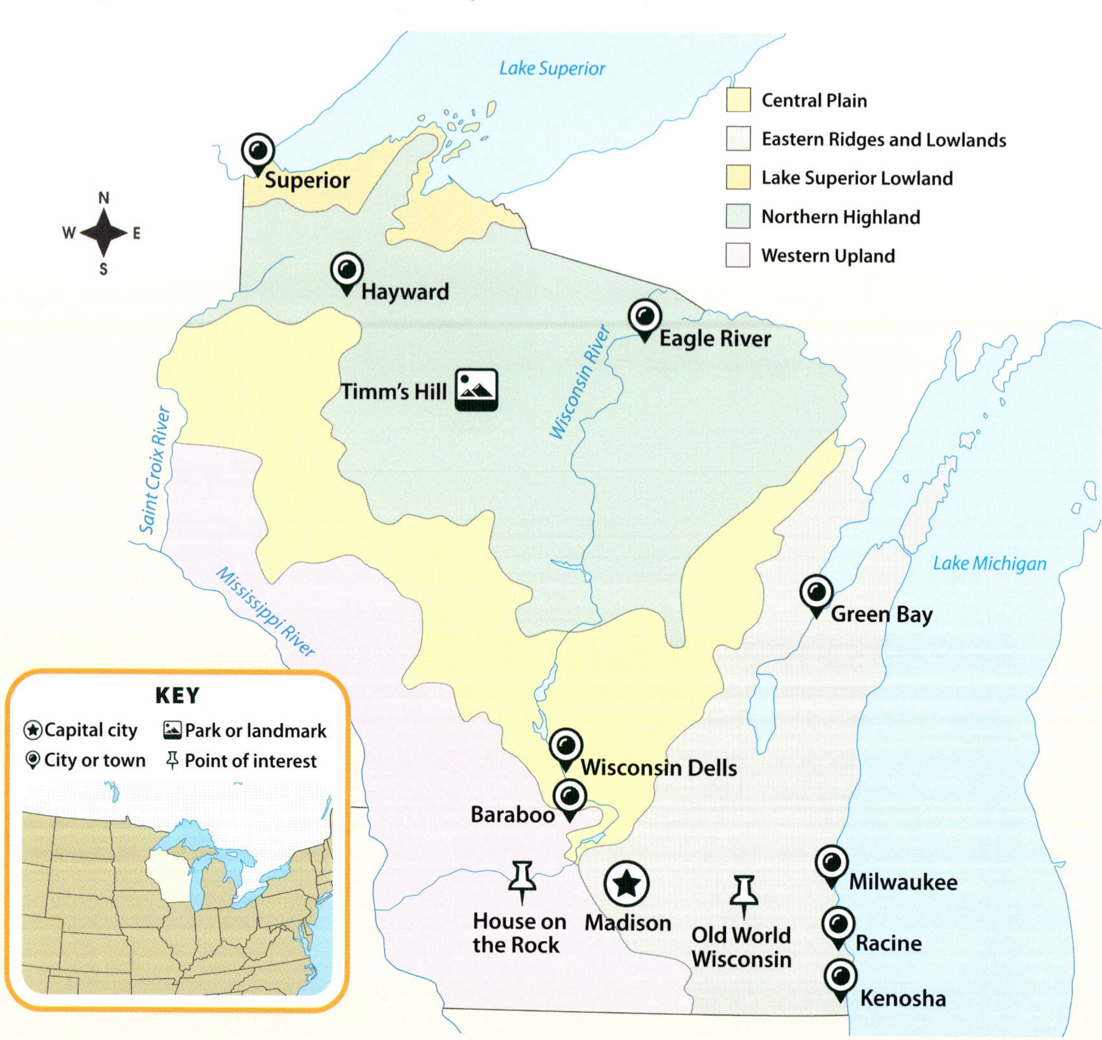

Much of central and southern Wisconsin is made up of farms and pastureland, while northern Wisconsin mainly consists of forests. Most of Wisconsin's large cities are located in the south and east. Madison is the state capital. It is located in the south-central region of the state. Milwaukee is the largest city. It is located along Lake Michigan. Cities along the Great Lakes such as Milwaukee, Green Bay, and Superior are important shipping centers. Other large cities include Kenosha and Racine.

Wisconsin is an amazing state with beautiful landscapes, unique history, and diverse people. It is unlike any other place in the country.

EXPLORE ONLINE

Chapter One discusses Wisconsin Dells. The website below goes into more depth on this topic. Does the website answer any questions you had about the town?

WISCONSIN DELLS HISTORY

abdocorelibrary.com/wisconsin

CHAPTER TWO

HISTORY OF WISCONSIN

People have lived in Wisconsin for at least 12,000 years. Over time the people formed several distinct nations. French explorer Jean Nicolet came to Wisconsin in 1634. The established American Indian peoples at that time included the Menominee, Ho-Chunk, and Dakota. Nicolet was the first European to arrive in Wisconsin, but he was quickly followed by French traders. The traders came to barter with the American Indians for furs.

The Menominee Indian Tribe of Wisconsin holds a powwow most years. Powwows celebrate American Indian cultures.

The French made alliances with the American Indian peoples and built trading posts along several of Wisconsin's rivers and lakes. Wars during the 1700s saw the land handed over first to Great Britain and then to the United States. As American settlers pushed west in search of land in the early 1800s, they forced many of Wisconsin's American Indian peoples from their homes.

STATEHOOD AND GOVERNMENT

Before Wisconsin became a state, it was a territory. The Wisconsin Territory was created in 1836. It included all of modern-day Wisconsin and parts of eastern Minnesota. Wisconsin became the thirtieth state on May 29, 1848. Much of its western border was set along the Mississippi and Saint Croix Rivers. Madison was its capital city. Wisconsin's state government was largely based on the US government. Today it has legislative, executive, and judicial branches to create, enforce, and interpret laws.

Wisconsin's state capitol building is located in Madison.

Wisconsin was formed as a free state. This meant that slavery was illegal. Many enslaved Black people from the Southern slave states fled north to escape slaveholders. They followed a transportation network known as the Underground Railroad. The cities of Milwaukee and Green Bay became stopping points along the Underground Railroad. People could find food, shelter, and passage to Canada at these cities. During the American Civil War (1861–1865), tens of thousands of soldiers from Wisconsin joined the fight against the proslavery Confederate States of America.

A LAND OF IMMIGRANTS

European immigrants were drawn to Wisconsin even before it was a state. The area's lead mines attracted British miners in the 1830s and 1840s. Germans also began settling in Wisconsin during that time. The geography and climate were similar to that of their homeland. A population boom in Scandinavia in the 1800s saw many Norwegian, Danish, and Swedish immigrants move to Wisconsin.

After Wisconsin became a state, its government began encouraging immigrants to move there. It printed flyers describing the opportunities for immigrants in Wisconsin. It sent the flyers to different countries in Europe. The state government also put ads in newspapers in American cities with large immigrant populations, such as New York City. Similarly, government labor programs helped bring thousands of people from Mexico, South America, and the Caribbean to Wisconsin in the mid-1900s.

RACIAL INJUSTICE

Some people have been treated unjustly throughout Wisconsin history. The US government tried to make American Indians more like white Americans. It made many American Indian children attend boarding schools from the late 1800s through the mid-1900s. Children were forced to speak only English at these schools. They could not speak their first languages. They were not allowed to practice their cultures. They had limited or no contact with their families. A growing number of people spoke against the schools in the early 1900s. The schools eventually closed. But they had caused

QUICK FACTS

Wisconsin's state symbols are uniquely suited to the state. Why do you think these symbols became a point of pride for Wisconsin?

Abbreviation: WI
Nickname: The Badger State
Motto: Forward
Date of Statehood: May 29, 1848
Capital: Madison
Population: 5,893,718
Area: 65,496 square miles (169,634 sq km)

STATE SYMBOLS

State animal
American badger

State dog
American water spaniel

State bird
American robin

State flower
Wood violet

many children to feel disconnected from their families and cultures.

Wisconsin has a long history of civil rights activism. Slavery was unpopular in many parts of the state. People in the state fought against the federal government's 1850 Fugitive Slave Act. The act required anyone who found escaped slaves to help return the enslaved people to the white slaveholders, even if they were found in

PERSPECTIVES

OJIBWE LANGUAGE SCHOOL

For more than 100 years, the US government tried to force American Indians in Wisconsin to assimilate, or conform, to American culture. American Indians had to learn the English language. Native languages were nearly lost as a result. In 2000 the Waadookodaading (wah-due-koh-dah-dihng) Ojibwe Language Immersion School opened in northwestern Wisconsin. The school teaches students to speak the Ojibwe language. Mark Montano is a member of the school board and the father of one of the school's students. He said in a 2019 interview, "It's important to me as a parent that [my son] knows who he is and where he comes from, and that's also supported by learning the language."

free states. In 1857 the Wisconsin state government passed a law that protected escaped slaves in the state from the Fugitive Slave Act. Then in 1895 the state passed a civil rights act banning segregation.

Many African Americans came to Wisconsin in the 1940s and 1950s. Most came to cities in the southeast part of the state, such as Milwaukee, for manufacturing jobs. But segregation still occurred despite the 1895 civil rights act. For example, some practices in Milwaukee kept Black people from living in certain areas. This created some neighborhoods with mostly white people. Other neighborhoods had mostly Black people. In the 1960s Black politicians Vel Phillips and Lloyd Barbee, along with Catholic priest James Groppi, led a civil rights movement in Wisconsin. They organized marches and protests against segregation, discrimination, and police violence. They also challenged these issues in the courts. People in Wisconsin continue to fight for civil rights today.

STRAIGHT TO THE
SOURCE

Carl De Haas immigrated to Wisconsin from Germany in 1847. He later published a guide to help other Germans immigrate to Wisconsin. In it he offered the following pieces of advice:

The man who comes with adequate resources, must not believe that he will be a rich man in a few years; he will make progress, soon be able to live without worries, and be able to look hopefully into the future, especially in regard to his children's future. But even this will only be true if he works hard. . . .

I am not saying that there are no other regions in America just as advantageous for settlement; . . . but I can assure you that there are few that are comparable in healthfulness, fertility and beauty of the land. . . . There is one more thing I wish to advise for everyone who plans to come over: he should learn something of the English language; . . . it will help him in America.

Source: Carl De Haas. *North America, Wisconsin, Hints for Emigrants*. J. Bädecker Verlag, 1848, pp. 41–42, books.google.com. Accessed 26 Jan. 2021.

WHAT'S THE BIG IDEA?

Read the above quote carefully. What are some of Haas's main points? Why does he feel that Wisconsin is better than other places in America? Why do you think his final piece of advice is to learn English?

GEOGRAPHY AND CLIMATE

Wisconsin has diverse geography. This is the result of the land once being partially covered by a glacier. As the glacier retreated, it smoothed the rough terrain and carved out lakes. It also churned the ground and created fertile soil. The last stage of the Ice Age in North America began approximately 100,000 years ago and ended around 18,000 years ago. It is known as the Wisconsin Glacial Stage. Although it affected much of North America, it was named

Wisconsin's fertile soil is good for growing crops and raising livestock.

after Wisconsin because geologists from the state first studied it.

Wisconsin is divided into five geographical regions. These regions are the Eastern Ridges and Lowlands, Central Plain, Northern Highland, Western Upland, and Lake Superior Lowland. Wisconsin's Central Plain is made up of grasslands with a few isolated hills. The Northern Highland is a hilly region dotted with thousands of lakes and wetlands. Much of the land is covered by trees. Timm's Hill is located there. It is Wisconsin's highest point, reaching 1,951 feet (595 m) above sea level.

Wisconsin's Eastern Ridges and Lowlands region borders Lake Michigan and consists of mostly flat plains. The plains are broken by the occasional steep ridge. This region contains most of Wisconsin's large cities. The Western Upland is made up of rugged hills and valleys with some forests. The Lake Superior Lowland is a mix of coastal plain and forested hills. Wisconsin includes more than 1,000 miles (1,600 km) of shoreline along Lake Superior and Lake Michigan. Many islands are scattered offshore.

CLIMATE

Wisconsin experiences four seasons. Summers are warm. Winters are cold and snowy with occasional blizzards. Yearly snowfall totals range from 40 inches (102 cm) to more than 100 inches (254 cm).

The climate along Lake Superior and Lake Michigan differs from the inland climate. Areas around the Great Lakes experience warmer temperatures than other

In the winter many people enjoy exploring the ice caves along Lake Superior.

parts of the state in the fall and winter. In the spring

and summer, the temperatures there are cooler than

elsewhere in Wisconsin. In winter cold air blowing over

the relatively warm waters of the lakes creates moisture.

This moisture can cause heavy snowfalls called lake-effect snow. Coasts along the Great Lakes can also experience strong winds as high as 65 miles per hour (105 km/h) in the fall and winter.

PLANTS AND ANIMALS

Wisconsin's northern woodlands and southern plains are home to a wide variety of plants and animals. Trees found in the northern woods include aspen, maple, and

PERSPECTIVES

INVASIVE SPECIES

Many invasive species have come to Wisconsin. These are species that are not native to the area. They compete with native species for food and disrupt the ecosystem. Zebra mussels, for example, were brought to the Great Lakes by cargo ships. Then they traveled to Wisconsin's inland lakes aboard smaller boats. Garlic mustard was brought by European immigrants as an herb. Invasive species can be hard to get rid of. Garlic mustard, according to Wisconsin Public Radio's Jill Nadeau, "can be like alien invaders in a bad sci-fi movie. It just keeps coming back—even after you think you've killed it off for good."

Parts of Wisconsin have rolling hills. Plowing this land in straight lines for crops causes a lot of soil to wash away with rainfall. People learned to care for the landscape by plowing strips of land along the side of a slope rather than strips that ran from the top to the bottom of the slope. The rows of crops kept soil from washing away.

red pine. The forests serve as habitat for many animals. White-tailed deer, gray wolves, bald eagles, and ruffed grouse live there. Waterfowl such as Canada geese and mallards live in Wisconsin's wetlands. The state's lakes and rivers are home to many species of fish, including walleye, northern pike, sturgeon, and trout. Wisconsin's southern plains have many grassland bird species, as well as deer and wild turkeys.

STRAIGHT TO THE
SOURCE

Aldo Leopold was an environmentalist. He worked in Wisconsin from the 1920s through the 1940s. He coined the term *the land ethic* in his 1949 book *A Sand County Almanac*. The land ethic is a view that people and the rest of nature are connected, like a community, and that people should treat the land with respect for mutual benefit. Leopold wrote in his book:

> *The land ethic simply enlarges the boundaries of the community to include soils, waters, plants, and animals, or collectively: the land. . . . In short, a land ethic changes the role of [humans] from conqueror of the land-community to plain member and citizen of it. It implies respect for his fellow-members, and also respect for the community as such.*

Source: Aldo Leopold. *A Sand County Almanac*. Oxford University, 2020, p. 192.

CONSIDER YOUR AUDIENCE

Review the above passage closely. Consider how you would adapt it for a different audience, such as your younger friends. Write a blog post conveying the new information so that it can be understood by them. How does your new approach differ from the original text, and why?

RESOURCES AND ECONOMY

he lumber industry was Wisconsin's first big industry. Northern Wisconsin was once covered with valuable white pine trees. They were cut into lumber and used for building projects around the country. The lumber boom began in the 1830s. It ended in the early 1900s when the seemingly endless white pines were mostly gone.

White pines still grow in the state today. Wisconsin's forests contain many other types of trees too. Logging continues to be an

Trees from Wisconsin are turned into products such as paper and lumber for construction.

important part of the state's economy. Wisconsin's trees are used mainly for making lumber, furniture, and paper.

Wisconsin is the top paper-producing state in the country. Mining is another important industry in Wisconsin. The state has many rich deposits of metals and minerals, including iron, lead, copper, and zinc.

Wisconsin has a thriving shipping industry. Because it borders Lake Superior and Lake Michigan, large quantities of goods are transported to and from the state over the water.

Cargo ships bring goods to and from Wisconsin at ports in cities including Green Bay.

Ships can travel across the Great Lakes and through the Saint Lawrence Seaway to the Atlantic Ocean. Wisconsin has several ports at Milwaukee, Green Bay, and Superior where cargo ships can dock. More than 42 million tons (38 million metric tons) of cargo pass through Wisconsin ports each year. The state exports goods such as machinery, vehicle parts, and farm products. It imports products including coal, cement, and oil.

Tourism brings billions of dollars into Wisconsin. Its many parks, lakes, and forests attract more than 100 million tourists from outside the state each year.

Tourism supports local businesses and generates millions of dollars in taxes.

FARMING

Wisconsin's fertile soil makes it ideal for farming. In 2020 there were more than 64,000 farms in the state. Wisconsin's main crops include grain, soybeans, potatoes, snap beans, and cranberries.

Wisconsin has more dairy farms than any other state. It is the country's top producer of cheese and the second-largest producer of milk. Wisconsin is famous for its cheese. Wisconsin cheesemakers produce more than 2 billion pounds (900 million kg) of cheese each year. They ship it to grocery stores and restaurants across the world.

Beef cattle are also raised for meat in Wisconsin. The large number of cattle created a large meatpacking industry in the 1850s. Meatpacking is the processing and packaging of meat. Green Bay's professional football team, the Green Bay Packers, was even named after it. But between the 1860s and 1920s, the meatpacking industry shifted to the western United States as cattle there increased in number.

FURTHER EVIDENCE

Chapter Four discusses how Wisconsin benefits from the Great Lakes. Identify one of the author's main points. What evidence does the author provide to support this point? The article at the website below also discusses the topic. Find a quote on this website that supports the author's main point. Does it offer a new piece of evidence?

THE GREAT LAKES SEAWAY PARTNERSHIP

abdocorelibrary.com/wisconsin

PEOPLE AND PLACES

The people of Wisconsin are known as Wisconsinites. The state's population was 5,893,718 in 2020. White people who are not Hispanic or Latino make up 90.9 percent of the population. The next largest racial groups are Hispanic and Latino at 7.1 percent and Black at 6.7 percent. The state also has 11 federally recognized American Indian tribes. These include the Ho-Chunk Nation and the Oneida Nation. These tribes have their own governments.

Milwaukee is Wisconsin's largest city.

In Milwaukee, students of the Dance Academy of Mexico learn Mexican folkloric and Aztec traditional dances.

Most people in Wisconsin live and work in large cities, such as Madison and Milwaukee. Others live in small towns and rural areas across the state. Milwaukee's population is 19 percent Latino. Some rural areas have even higher percentages of Latinos. Here, many work in agriculture.

Famous Wisconsinites include actor Mark Ruffalo, pro basketball player Arike Ogunbowale, and pro football player J. J. Watt. Writer Laura Ingalls Wilder was also from Wisconsin. Her childhood home in Pepin County was the setting for her 1932 book *Little House in the Big Woods*. Later she wrote her most famous book, *Little House on the Prairie*.

PLACES

Many people visit Madison and Milwaukee for their museums, theaters, food, and sports venues. Because of

PERSPECTIVES

GEORGE POAGE

George Coleman Poage was a famous Black athlete who grew up in La Crosse, Wisconsin, in the late 1800s. He was the first Black athlete to run for the University of Wisconsin's track team. He went on to compete in the 1904 Olympic games. There he became the first Black American to win an Olympic medal. In 2013 the city of La Crosse named a park after Poage. Steve Carlyon, La Crosse's director of parks and recreation, said in a 2016 interview: "The whole message of the park is to create hope for young men and women."

Packers players often celebrate touchdowns by jumping up to
the fans in a move known as the Lambeau Leap.

Milwaukee's large Latino population, many people get

to enjoy dining at authentic Latin American restaurants

in the city. American Family Field is located in

Milwaukee. It is the ballpark of the Milwaukee Brewers

baseball team. Green Bay's Lambeau Field is another

popular destination. It is the home of the Green Bay Packers football team.

There is a lot to see and do outside of the big cities as well. Old World Wisconsin, near Eagle, is an outdoor museum. Costumed staff demonstrate settler life in the 1800s. Thousands of people visit the House on the Rock each year to see its unique collection of art and historical objects. There are also two national parks and more than 40 state parks in the state. People camp, hike, and ski at these places. Hunters go to Wisconsin's northern woods because of the abundant white-tailed deer, grouse, and waterfowl. The state's many lakes and rivers are great for fishing. People also visit the sand and stone beaches along Lake Superior and Lake Michigan.

Wisconsin has many large outdoor festivals. Each summer Milwaukee hosts Summerfest, a large music festival. Wisconsin has the third-largest Hmong population in the country. Every December Milwaukee hosts a large Hmong new year celebration that lasts two days. American Indians celebrate their cultures and traditions at powwows held throughout Wisconsin. At powwows, American Indians sing songs and perform dances that have been tied to their nations for generations. Some people sing songs in their native languages.

Oshkosh is home to the world's largest aviation show. People race snowmobiles at the World Championship Snowmobile Derby in Eagle River. The Lumberjack World Championships are held in Hayward. People compete in timber sports such as log rolling,

People from around the country and world compete in the Lumberjack World Championships.

tree chopping, and axe throwing. Wisconsinites are proud to celebrate the history, beauty, and cultures that make up their state.

IMPORTANT DATES

12,000 years ago

People first inhabit Wisconsin at this time, if not earlier.

1634

French explorer Jean Nicolet becomes the first European to visit Wisconsin.

1836

The Wisconsin Territory is established.

1848

Wisconsin becomes the thirtieth state on May 29.

1861–1865

Tens of thousands of people in Wisconsin enlist to fight in the American Civil War.

1895

The Wisconsin state government passes a civil rights act banning segregation.

1960s

Vel Phillips, Lloyd Barbee, and James Groppi help lead the civil rights movement in Wisconsin.

2016

A memorial to Hmong Vietnam War veterans is erected in Wausau.

2020

Wisconsin has more than 64,000 farms.

Surprise Me

Chapter Five discusses people and places in Wisconsin. After reading this book, what two or three facts about Wisconsin did you find most surprising? Write a few sentences about each fact. Why did you find each fact surprising?

Dig Deeper

After reading this book, what questions do you still have about the climate in Wisconsin? With an adult's help, find a few reliable sources that can help you answer your questions. Write a paragraph about what you learned.

Take a Stand

Some people visit Wisconsin Dells for the water parks. Others visit for its natural beauty. Do you find one of these features more impressive than the other? Or do you think both are equally important? Explain your answer.

You Are There

Chapter Three discusses geography, plants, and wildlife in Wisconsin. Imagine you are traveling to Wisconsin. Write a letter home telling your friends what you see. What do you notice about the different kinds of land? What animals live in each place? Be sure to add plenty of detail to your notes.

GLOSSARY

artificial
made by humans

bluff
a steep bank along a body
of water

economy
a place's system of goods,
services, money, and jobs

export
to ship and sell products to
another region or country

import
to buy and bring in products
from another region
or country

segregation
the separation of groups of
people based on race, class,
or ethnicity

tax
money gathered by a
government from its people

wetland
an area of land with a lot
of water, such as a marsh
or swamp

ONLINE RESOURCES

To learn more about Wisconsin, visit our free resource websites below.

Visit **abdocorelibrary.com** or scan this QR code for free Common Core resources for teachers and students, including vetted activities, multimedia, and booklinks, for deeper subject comprehension.

Visit **abdobooklinks.com** or scan this QR code for free additional online weblinks for further learning. These links are routinely monitored and updated to provide the most current information available.

LEARN MORE

Hunter, Tony. *Green Bay Packers*. Abdo, 2020.

Micklos, John, Jr. *Wisconsin*. Cavendish Square, 2019.

Porter, Adele. *Wild about Wisconsin Birds*. Adventure Publications, 2019.

INDEX

About the Author

Ryan Gale is an artist and writer from Minnesota. He enjoys visiting his neighboring state of Wisconsin.